The Evergreen Pacific LOG BOOK

Walker Common Sense Edition

**The Evergreen Pacific Log Book:
Walker Common Sense Edition**
Copyright © 1990 Milo and Terri Walker
**Reprinted 1994, 1995, 1996, 1997,
1998, 2000 (with minor revisions),
2001, 2002, 2003, 2004, 2005 & 2006**

Evergreen Pacific
Publishing Ltd.
4204 Russell Road, Suite M
Mukilteo, WA 98275
www.evergreenpacific.com

ISBN 0-945265-31-X

Printed in Hong Kong

TABLE OF CONTENTS

INTRODUCING

Walker's "Common Sense" Log Book

After many years of owning and operating various boats, we have found one continuing frustration — finding a log book that makes sense to the average boat owner. Unable to find one to suit our needs, we did what most others do—adapt other log books to meet our needs. Over the last five years we discussed the need for a basic log book with many boaters, and, like them, waited for someone to do something about it. Understanding finally dawned that we were waiting for something that wouldn't happen unless we did it ourselves, so here is the Walker Common Sense Edition of a log book.

This log book contains the basic information every boater should know, along with clear, concise, TABBED sections for vessel, fuel, maintenance, inventory, and radio log records. Most important, however, is the daily log. It contains enough room to record your adventures in depth, so that years from now you will be able to look back and fondly remember the good (and bad) times. A daily log does not have to be an impersonal collection of vessel and marine-related data.

This book is created as a PERSONAL log, to keep in your own library, not to be transferred with the boat. It is, however, designed so the vessel records can be easily photocopied for the next owner without passing on your personal journal. Thus, the resale value of your boat increases as it does with any property sold with complete records. You can keep your memories and you can have important vessel documentation.

We firmly believe this is the "Common Sense" log book average boaters have been waiting for. So, without further ado, we wish you good boating and fond memories. Bon Voyage!

Milo and Terri Walker

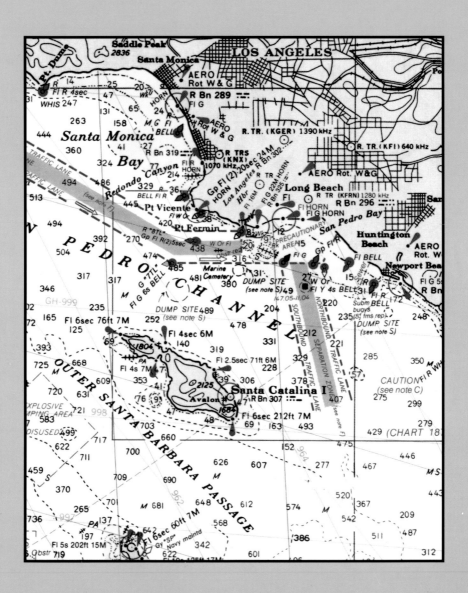

VESSEL INFORMATION

Name _____ Hailing Port _____

I.D. Number _____ Radio Call Sign _____

Owner's Name _____ Telephone Number (_____) _____

Address _____

Builder _____ Model _____

Year _____ Length _____ Draft _____ Beam _____

Height _____ Hull Color _____ Trim Color _____

Number of Masts _____ Mast Height(s) _____

Propeller Size(s) _____ Rotation _____

Vessel Construction Material _____

Engine Make(s) _____ Engine Model(s) _____

Serial Number(s) _____ Number of Cylinders (per) _____

Oil Type Winter _____ Summer _____

Fuel Tank(s) Capacity _____ Water Tank(s) Capacity _____

Hot Water Tank Capacity _____ Generator Make/Model _____

Transmission Type _____ Transmission Model _____ Transmission Oil _____

Insurance Company _____ Telephone Number (_____) _____

Address _____

Policy Number _____ Agent _____

1

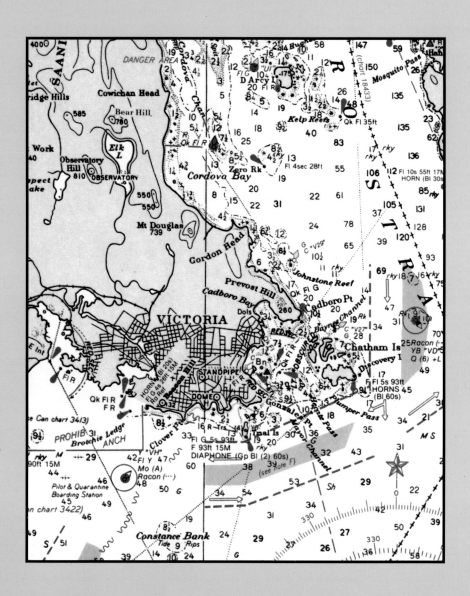

DAILY CRUISING LOG

Date	Time Start	Time Finish	Cruise From	Cruise To

Engine Hours		Gen-Set Hours		Engine	Weather/Sea Conditions
Start	Finish	Start	Finish	Avg. RPMs	

JOURNAL

DAILY CRUISING LOG

Date	Time Start	Time Finish	Cruise From	Cruise To

Engine Hours		Gen-Set Hours		Engine	Weather/Sea Conditions
Start	Finish	Start	Finish	Avg. RPMs	

JOURNAL

DAILY CRUISING LOG

Date	Time Start	Time Finish	Cruise From	Cruise To

Engine Hours		Gen-Set Hours		Engine	Weather/Sea Conditions
Start	Finish	Start	Finish	Avg. RPMs	

JOURNAL

DAILY CRUISING LOG

Date	Time Start	Time Finish	Cruise From	Cruise To

Engine Hours		Gen-Set Hours		Engine	Weather/Sea Conditions
Start	Finish	Start	Finish	Avg. RPMs	

JOURNAL

DAILY CRUISING LOG

Date	Time Start	Time Finish	Cruise From	Cruise To

Engine Hours		Gen-Set Hours		Engine	Weather/Sea Conditions
Start	Finish	Start	Finish	Avg. RPMs	

JOURNAL

DAILY CRUISING LOG

Date	Time Start	Time Finish	Cruise From	Cruise To

Engine Hours		Gen-Set Hours		Engine	Weather/Sea Conditions
Start	Finish	Start	Finish	Avg. RPMs	

JOURNAL

DAILY CRUISING LOG

Date	Time Start	Time Finish	Cruise From	Cruise To

Engine Hours		Gen-Set Hours		Engine	Weather/Sea Conditions
Start	Finish	Start	Finish	Avg. RPMs	

JOURNAL

DAILY CRUISING LOG

Date	Time Start	Time Finish	Cruise From	Cruise To

Engine Hours		Gen-Set Hours		Engine	Weather/Sea Conditions
Start	Finish	Start	Finish	Avg. RPMs	

JOURNAL

DAILY CRUISING LOG

Date	Time Start	Time Finish	Cruise From	Cruise To

Engine Hours		Gen-Set Hours		Engine	Weather/Sea Conditions
Start	Finish	Start	Finish	Avg. RPMs	

JOURNAL

DAILY CRUISING LOG

Date	Time Start	Time Finish	Cruise From	Cruise To

Engine Hours		Gen-Set Hours		Engine	Weather/Sea Conditions
Start	Finish	Start	Finish	Avg. RPMs	

JOURNAL

DAILY CRUISING LOG

Date	Time Start	Time Finish	Cruise From	Cruise To

Engine Hours		Gen-Set Hours		Engine	Weather/Sea Conditions
Start	Finish	Start	Finish	Avg. RPMs	

JOURNAL

DAILY CRUISING LOG

Date	Time Start	Time Finish	Cruise From	Cruise To

Engine Hours		Gen-Set Hours		Engine	Weather/Sea Conditions
Start	Finish	Start	Finish	Avg. RPMs	

JOURNAL

DAILY CRUISING LOG

Date	Time Start	Time Finish	Cruise From	Cruise To

Engine Hours		Gen-Set Hours		Engine	Weather/Sea Conditions
Start	Finish	Start	Finish	Avg. RPMs	

JOURNAL

DAILY CRUISING LOG

Date	Time Start	Time Finish	Cruise From	Cruise To

Engine Hours		Gen-Set Hours		Engine	Weather/Sea Conditions
Start	Finish	Start	Finish	Avg. RPMs	

JOURNAL

blank lined journal area

DAILY CRUISING LOG

Date	Time Start	Time Finish	Cruise From	Cruise To

Engine Hours		Gen-Set Hours		Engine	Weather/Sea Conditions
Start	Finish	Start	Finish	Avg. RPMs	

JOURNAL

DAILY CRUISING LOG

Date	Time Start	Time Finish	Cruise From	Cruise To

Engine Hours		Gen-Set Hours		Engine	Weather/Sea Conditions
Start	Finish	Start	Finish	Avg. RPMs	

JOURNAL

DAILY CRUISING LOG

Date	Time Start	Time Finish	Cruise From	Cruise To

Engine Hours		Gen-Set Hours		Engine	Weather/Sea Conditions
Start	Finish	Start	Finish	Avg. RPMs	

JOURNAL

DAILY CRUISING LOG

Date	Time Start	Time Finish	Cruise From	Cruise To

Engine Hours		Gen-Set Hours		Engine	Weather/Sea Conditions
Start	Finish	Start	Finish	Avg. RPMs	

JOURNAL

DAILY CRUISING LOG

Date	Time Start	Time Finish	Cruise From	Cruise To

Engine Hours		Gen-Set Hours		Engine	Weather/Sea Conditions
Start	Finish	Start	Finish	Avg. RPMs	

JOURNAL

DAILY CRUISING LOG

Date	Time Start	Time Finish	Cruise From	Cruise To

Engine Hours		Gen-Set Hours		Engine	Weather/Sea Conditions
Start	Finish	Start	Finish	Avg. RPMs	

JOURNAL

DAILY CRUISING LOG

Date	Time Start	Time Finish	Cruise From	Cruise To

Engine Hours		Gen-Set Hours		Engine	Weather/Sea Conditions
Start	Finish	Start	Finish	Avg. RPMs	

JOURNAL

DAILY CRUISING LOG

Date	Time Start	Time Finish	Cruise From	Cruise To

Engine Hours		Gen-Set Hours		Engine	Weather/Sea Conditions
Start	Finish	Start	Finish	Avg. RPMs	

JOURNAL

DAILY CRUISING LOG

Date	Time Start	Time Finish	Cruise From	Cruise To

Engine Hours		Gen-Set Hours		Engine	Weather/Sea Conditions
Start	Finish	Start	Finish	Avg. RPMs	

JOURNAL

DAILY CRUISING LOG

Date	Time Start	Time Finish	Cruise From	Cruise To

Engine Hours		Gen-Set Hours		Engine	Weather/Sea Conditions
Start	Finish	Start	Finish	Avg. RPMs	

JOURNAL

DAILY CRUISING LOG

Date	Time Start	Time Finish	Cruise From	Cruise To

Engine Hours		Gen-Set Hours		Engine	Weather/Sea Conditions
Start	Finish	Start	Finish	Avg. RPMs	

JOURNAL

DAILY CRUISING LOG

Date	Time Start	Time Finish	Cruise From	Cruise To

Engine Hours		Gen-Set Hours		Engine	Weather/Sea Conditions
Start	Finish	Start	Finish	Avg. RPMs	

JOURNAL

DAILY CRUISING LOG

Date	Time Start	Time Finish	Cruise From	Cruise To

Engine Hours		Gen-Set Hours		Engine	Weather/Sea Conditions
Start	Finish	Start	Finish	Avg. RPMs	

JOURNAL

DAILY CRUISING LOG

Date	Time Start	Time Finish	Cruise From	Cruise To

Engine Hours		Gen-Set Hours		Engine	Weather/Sea Conditions
Start	Finish	Start	Finish	Avg. RPMs	

JOURNAL

DAILY CRUISING LOG

Date	Time Start	Time Finish	Cruise From	Cruise To

Engine Hours		Gen-Set Hours		Engine	Weather/Sea Conditions
Start	Finish	Start	Finish	Avg. RPMs	

JOURNAL

DAILY CRUISING LOG

Date	Time Start	Time Finish	Cruise From	Cruise To

Engine Hours		Gen-Set Hours		Engine	Weather/Sea Conditions
Start	Finish	Start	Finish	Avg. RPMs	

JOURNAL

DAILY CRUISING LOG

Date	Time Start	Time Finish	Cruise From	Cruise To

Engine Hours		Gen-Set Hours		Engine	Weather/Sea Conditions
Start	Finish	Start	Finish	Avg. RPMs	

JOURNAL

DAILY CRUISING LOG

Date	Time Start	Time Finish	Cruise From	Cruise To

Engine Hours		Gen-Set Hours		Engine	Weather/Sea Conditions
Start	Finish	Start	Finish	Avg. RPMs	

JOURNAL

DAILY CRUISING LOG

Date	Time Start	Time Finish	Cruise From	Cruise To

Engine Hours		Gen-Set Hours		Engine	Weather/Sea Conditions
Start	Finish	Start	Finish	Avg. RPMs	

JOURNAL

DAILY CRUISING LOG

Date	Time Start	Time Finish	Cruise From	Cruise To

Engine Hours		Gen-Set Hours		Engine	Weather/Sea Conditions
Start	Finish	Start	Finish	Avg. RPMs	

JOURNAL

DAILY CRUISING LOG

Date	Time Start	Time Finish	Cruise From	Cruise To

Engine Hours		Gen-Set Hours		Engine	Weather/Sea Conditions
Start	Finish	Start	Finish	Avg. RPMs	

JOURNAL

DAILY CRUISING LOG

Date	Time Start	Time Finish	Cruise From	Cruise To

Engine Hours		Gen-Set Hours		Engine	Weather/Sea Conditions
Start	Finish	Start	Finish	Avg. RPMs	

JOURNAL

DAILY CRUISING LOG

Date	Time Start	Time Finish	Cruise From	Cruise To

Engine Hours		Gen-Set Hours		Engine	Weather/Sea Conditions
Start	Finish	Start	Finish	Avg. RPMs	

JOURNAL

DAILY CRUISING LOG

Date	Time Start	Time Finish	Cruise From	Cruise To

Engine Hours		Gen-Set Hours		Engine	Weather/Sea Conditions
Start	Finish	Start	Finish	Avg. RPMs	

JOURNAL

DAILY CRUISING LOG

Date	Time Start	Time Finish	Cruise From	Cruise To

Engine Hours		Gen-Set Hours		Engine	Weather/Sea Conditions
Start	Finish	Start	Finish	Avg. RPMs	

JOURNAL

DAILY CRUISING LOG

Date	Time Start	Time Finish	Cruise From	Cruise To

Engine Hours		Gen-Set Hours		Engine	Weather/Sea Conditions
Start	Finish	Start	Finish	Avg. RPMs	

JOURNAL

DAILY CRUISING LOG

Date	Time Start	Time Finish	Cruise From	Cruise To

Engine Hours		Gen-Set Hours		Engine	Weather/Sea Conditions
Start	Finish	Start	Finish	Avg. RPMs	

JOURNAL

DAILY CRUISING LOG

Date	Time Start	Time Finish	Cruise From	Cruise To

Engine Hours		Gen-Set Hours		Engine	Weather/Sea Conditions
Start	Finish	Start	Finish	Avg. RPMs	

JOURNAL

DAILY CRUISING LOG

Date	Time Start	Time Finish	Cruise From	Cruise To

Engine Hours		Gen-Set Hours		Engine	Weather/Sea Conditions
Start	Finish	Start	Finish	Avg. RPMs	

JOURNAL

DAILY CRUISING LOG

Date	Time Start	Time Finish	Cruise From	Cruise To

Engine Hours		Gen-Set Hours		Engine	Weather/Sea Conditions
Start	Finish	Start	Finish	Avg. RPMs	

JOURNAL

DAILY CRUISING LOG

Date	Time Start	Time Finish	Cruise From	Cruise To

Engine Hours		Gen-Set Hours		Engine	Weather/Sea Conditions
Start	Finish	Start	Finish	Avg. RPMs	

JOURNAL

DAILY CRUISING LOG

Date	Time Start	Time Finish	Cruise From	Cruise To

Engine Hours		Gen-Set Hours		Engine	Weather/Sea Conditions
Start	Finish	Start	Finish	Avg. RPMs	

JOURNAL

DAILY CRUISING LOG

Date	Time Start	Time Finish	Cruise From	Cruise To

Engine Hours		Gen-Set Hours		Engine	Weather/Sea Conditions
Start	Finish	Start	Finish	Avg. RPMs	

JOURNAL

DAILY CRUISING LOG

Date	Time Start	Time Finish	Cruise From	Cruise To

Engine Hours		Gen-Set Hours		Engine	Weather/Sea Conditions
Start	Finish	Start	Finish	Avg. RPMs	

JOURNAL

DAILY CRUISING LOG

Date	Time Start	Time Finish	Cruise From	Cruise To

Engine Hours		Gen-Set Hours		Engine	Weather/Sea Conditions
Start	Finish	Start	Finish	Avg. RPMs	

JOURNAL

DAILY CRUISING LOG

Date	Time Start	Time Finish	Cruise From	Cruise To

Engine Hours		Gen-Set Hours		Engine	Weather/Sea Conditions
Start	Finish	Start	Finish	Avg. RPMs	

JOURNAL

DAILY CRUISING LOG

Date	Time Start	Time Finish	Cruise From	Cruise To

Engine Hours		Gen-Set Hours		Engine	Weather/Sea Conditions
Start	Finish	Start	Finish	Avg. RPMs	

JOURNAL

DAILY CRUISING LOG

Date	Time Start	Time Finish	Cruise From	Cruise To

Engine Hours		Gen-Set Hours		Engine	Weather/Sea Conditions
Start	Finish	Start	Finish	Avg. RPMs	

JOURNAL

DAILY CRUISING LOG

Date	Time Start	Time Finish	Cruise From	Cruise To

Engine Hours		Gen-Set Hours		Engine	Weather/Sea Conditions
Start	Finish	Start	Finish	Avg. RPMs	

JOURNAL

DAILY CRUISING LOG

Date	Time Start	Time Finish	Cruise From	Cruise To

Engine Hours		Gen-Set Hours		Engine	Weather/Sea Conditions
Start	Finish	Start	Finish	Avg. RPMs	

JOURNAL

DAILY CRUISING LOG

Date	Time Start	Time Finish	Cruise From	Cruise To

Engine Hours		Gen-Set Hours		Engine	Weather/Sea Conditions
Start	Finish	Start	Finish	Avg. RPMs	

JOURNAL

DAILY CRUISING LOG

Date	Time Start	Time Finish	Cruise From	Cruise To

Engine Hours		Gen-Set Hours		Engine	Weather/Sea Conditions
Start	Finish	Start	Finish	Avg. RPMs	

JOURNAL

DAILY CRUISING LOG

Date	Time Start	Time Finish	Cruise From		Cruise To

Engine Hours		Gen-Set Hours		Engine	Weather/Sea Conditions
Start	Finish	Start	Finish	Avg. RPMs	

JOURNAL

DAILY CRUISING LOG

Date	Time Start	Time Finish	Cruise From	Cruise To

Engine Hours		Gen-Set Hours		Engine	Weather/Sea Conditions
Start	Finish	Start	Finish	Avg. RPMs	

JOURNAL

DAILY CRUISING LOG

Date	Time Start	Time Finish	Cruise From	Cruise To

Engine Hours		Gen-Set Hours		Engine	Weather/Sea Conditions
Start	Finish	Start	Finish	Avg. RPMs	

JOURNAL

DAILY CRUISING LOG

Date	Time Start	Time Finish	Cruise From	Cruise To

Engine Hours		Gen-Set Hours		Engine	Weather/Sea Conditions
Start	Finish	Start	Finish	Avg. RPMs	

JOURNAL

DAILY CRUISING LOG

Date	Time Start	Time Finish	Cruise From	Cruise To

Engine Hours		Gen-Set Hours		Engine	Weather/Sea Conditions
Start	Finish	Start	Finish	Avg. RPMs	

JOURNAL

DAILY CRUISING LOG

Date	Time Start	Time Finish	Cruise From	Cruise To

Engine Hours		Gen-Set Hours		Engine	Weather/Sea Conditions
Start	Finish	Start	Finish	Avg. RPMs	

JOURNAL

DAILY CRUISING LOG

Date	Time Start	Time Finish	Cruise From	Cruise To

Engine Hours		Gen-Set Hours		Engine	Weather/Sea Conditions
Start	Finish	Start	Finish	Avg. RPMs	

JOURNAL

DAILY CRUISING LOG

Date	Time Start	Time Finish	Cruise From	Cruise To

Engine Hours		Gen-Set Hours		Engine	Weather/Sea Conditions
Start	Finish	Start	Finish	Avg. RPMs	

JOURNAL

DAILY CRUISING LOG

Date	Time Start	Time Finish	Cruise From	Cruise To

Engine Hours		Gen-Set Hours		Engine	Weather/Sea Conditions
Start	Finish	Start	Finish	Avg. RPMs	

JOURNAL

DAILY CRUISING LOG

Date	Time Start	Time Finish	Cruise From	Cruise To

Engine Hours		Gen-Set Hours		Engine	Weather/Sea Conditions
Start	Finish	Start	Finish	Avg. RPMs	

JOURNAL

DAILY CRUISING LOG

Date	Time Start	Time Finish	Cruise From	Cruise To

Engine Hours		Gen-Set Hours		Engine	Weather/Sea Conditions
Start	Finish	Start	Finish	Avg. RPMs	

JOURNAL

DAILY CRUISING LOG

Date	Time Start	Time Finish	Cruise From	Cruise To

Engine Hours		Gen-Set Hours		Engine	Weather/Sea Conditions
Start	Finish	Start	Finish	Avg. RPMs	

JOURNAL

DAILY CRUISING LOG

Date	Time Start	Time Finish	Cruise From	Cruise To

Engine Hours		Gen-Set Hours		Engine	Weather/Sea Conditions
Start	Finish	Start	Finish	Avg. RPMs	

JOURNAL

DAILY CRUISING LOG

Date	Time Start	Time Finish	Cruise From	Cruise To

Engine Hours		Gen-Set Hours		Engine	Weather/Sea Conditions
Start	Finish	Start	Finish	Avg. RPMs	

JOURNAL

DAILY CRUISING LOG

Date	Time Start	Time Finish	Cruise From	Cruise To

Engine Hours		Gen-Set Hours		Engine	Weather/Sea Conditions
Start	Finish	Start	Finish	Avg. RPMs	

JOURNAL

DAILY CRUISING LOG

Date	Time Start	Time Finish	Cruise From	Cruise To

Engine Hours		Gen-Set Hours		Engine	Weather/Sea Conditions
Start	Finish	Start	Finish	Avg. RPMs	

JOURNAL

DAILY CRUISING LOG

Date	Time Start	Time Finish	Cruise From	Cruise To

Engine Hours		Gen-Set Hours		Engine	Weather/Sea Conditions
Start	Finish	Start	Finish	Avg. RPMs	

JOURNAL

DAILY CRUISING LOG

Date	Time Start	Time Finish	Cruise From	Cruise To

Engine Hours		Gen-Set Hours		Engine	Weather/Sea Conditions
Start	Finish	Start	Finish	Avg. RPMs	

JOURNAL

DAILY CRUISING LOG

Date	Time Start	Time Finish	Cruise From	Cruise To

Engine Hours		Gen-Set Hours		Engine	Weather/Sea Conditions
Start	Finish	Start	Finish	Avg. RPMs	

JOURNAL

DAILY CRUISING LOG

Date	Time Start	Time Finish	Cruise From	Cruise To

| Engine Hours | | Gen-Set Hours | | Engine | Weather/Sea Conditions |
Start	Finish	Start	Finish	Avg. RPMs	

JOURNAL

DAILY CRUISING LOG

Date	Time Start	Time Finish	Cruise From	Cruise To

Engine Hours		Gen-Set Hours		Engine	Weather/Sea Conditions
Start	Finish	Start	Finish	Avg. RPMs	

JOURNAL

DAILY CRUISING LOG

Date	Time Start	Time Finish	Cruise From	Cruise To

Engine Hours		Gen-Set Hours		Engine	Weather/Sea Conditions
Start	Finish	Start	Finish	Avg. RPMs	

JOURNAL

DAILY CRUISING LOG

Date	Time Start	Time Finish	Cruise From	Cruise To

Engine Hours		Gen-Set Hours		Engine	Weather/Sea Conditions
Start	Finish	Start	Finish	Avg. RPMs	

JOURNAL

DAILY CRUISING LOG

Date	Time Start	Time Finish	Cruise From	Cruise To

Engine Hours		Gen-Set Hours		Engine	Weather/Sea Conditions
Start	Finish	Start	Finish	Avg. RPMs	

JOURNAL

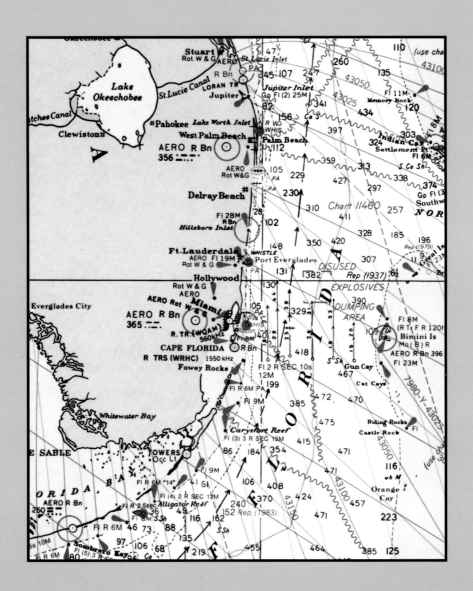

FUEL LOG

Date	Location	Engine Hours	Cost Per Gallon	Total Gallons	Total Cost	GPH *	Comments

* To calculate gallons per hours = hours $\sqrt{\,}$ gallons.

FUEL LOG

Date	Location	Engine Hours	Cost Per Gallon	Total Gallons	Total Cost	GPH *	Comments

* To calculate gallons per hours = hours $\sqrt{\text{gallons}}$.

FUEL LOG

Date	Location	Engine Hours	Cost Per Gallon	Total Gallons	Total Cost	GPH *	Comments

* To calculate gallons per hours = hours $\sqrt{\text{gallons}}$.

FUEL LOG

Date	Location	Engine Hours	Cost Per Gallon	Total Gallons	Total Cost	GPH *	Comments

* To calculate gallons per hours = hours $\sqrt{\text{gallons}}$.

FUEL LOG

Date	Location	Engine Hours	Cost Per Gallon	Total Gallons	Total Cost	GPH *	Comments

* To calculate gallons per hours = hours $\sqrt{}$ gallons.

FUEL LOG

Date	Location	Engine Hours	Cost Per Gallon	Total Gallons	Total Cost	GPH *	Comments

* To calculate gallons per hours = hours $\sqrt{\text{gallons}}$.

FUEL LOG

Date	Location	Engine Hours	Cost Per Gallon	Total Gallons	Total Cost	GPH *	Comments

* To calculate gallons per hours = hours $\sqrt{\text{gallons}}$.

FUEL LOG

Date	Location	Engine Hours	Cost Per Gallon	Total Gallons	Total Cost	GPH *	Comments

* To calculate gallons per hours = hours $\sqrt{\text{gallons}}$.

FUEL LOG

Date	Location	Engine Hours	Cost Per Gallon	Total Gallons	Total Cost	GPH *	Comments

* To calculate gallons per hours = hours $\sqrt{\text{gallons}}$.

FUEL LOG

Date	Location	Engine Hours	Cost Per Gallon	Total Gallons	Total Cost	GPH *	Comments

* To calculate gallons per hours = hours $\sqrt{\text{gallons}}$.

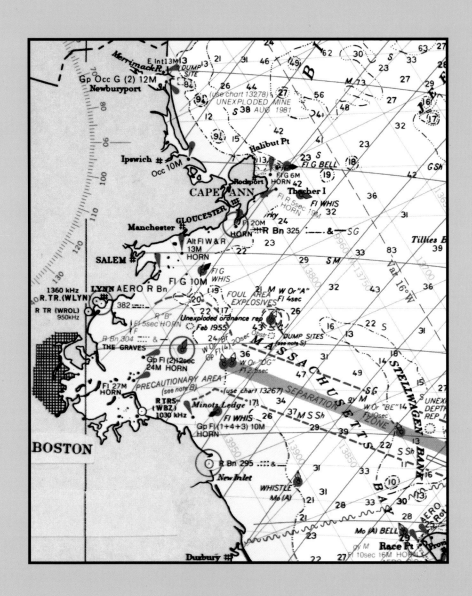

MAINTENANCE LOG

Date	Engine Hours	Location	Cost	Description / Comments

MAINTENANCE LOG

Date	Engine Hours	Location	Cost	Description / Comments

MAINTENANCE LOG

Date	Engine Hours	Location	Cost	Description / Comments

MAINTENANCE LOG

Date	Engine Hours	Location	Cost	Description / Comments

MAINTENANCE LOG

Date	Engine Hours	Location	Cost	Description / Comments

MAINTENANCE LOG

Date	Engine Hours	Location	Cost	Description / Comments

MAINTENANCE LOG

Date	Engine Hours	Location	Cost	Description / Comments

MAINTENANCE LOG

Date	Engine Hours	Location	Cost	Description / Comments

MAINTENANCE LOG

Date	Engine Hours	Location	Cost	Description / Comments

MAINTENANCE LOG

Date	Engine Hours	Location	Cost	Description / Comments

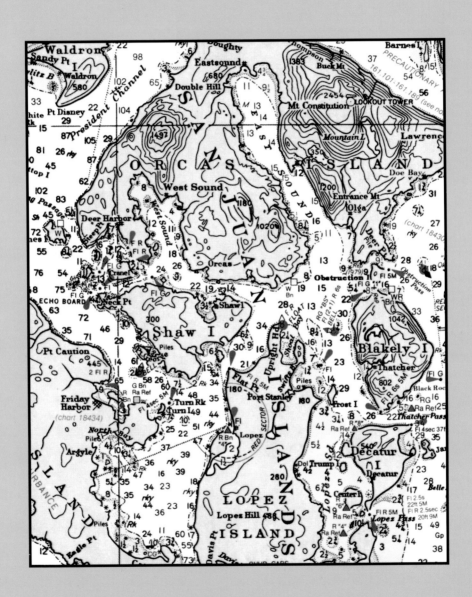

EMERGENCY "MAYDAY" INFORMATION

These instruction are to be used and followed **ONLY** when there is **IMMEDIATE** danger of loss to life or property. *

When it is necessary to use this distress signal speak:

SLOWLY — CLEARLY — CALMLY

1. Turn radio-telephone on, to VHF channel 16 (156.8 HRz) or 2182 KHz, whichever channel applies.

2. Repeat: "MAYDAY — MAYDAY — MAYDAY."

3. Give your **RADIO CALL SIGN** (three times) followed by the **NAME** of your **VESSEL** (repeated three times).

4. Give your **POSITION** as best you can, describing any significant landmarks.

5. State the **NATURE** of your **DISTRESS** (e.g., vessel sinking, need medical assistance, etc.).

6. State **NUMBER** of **ADULTS** and **CHILDREN** on board and conditions of injured.

7. State **SEAWORTHINESS** of **VESSEL** (e.g., engine out, taking on water, etc.).

8. **DESCRIBE** your **VESSEL** for quick identification to searchers.

9. **GIVE** radio frequency channel you will be listening to, with a monitoring schedule (e.g., "I will be listening on channel 16 every fifteen minutes.").

10. Wait for response and reply accordingly.

* **NOTE**: All vessels should have on board the "MARINE RADIO PROCEDURES GUIDE" published by Technical Information Services, distributed by most local marine stores.

RADIO LOG

Vessel Name _____   Radio Call Sign _____

Coast Guard VHF Radio Requirements:
1. Must enter each distress (Mayday) message sent **OR** heard.
2. Must enter each urgency (Panpan) for safety (Security) message **you** send.
3. Must enter data on installation and servicing of radio.
4. All entries must be signed by operator.
5. Must retain Radio Log one year minimum from last entry.

Date	Time	Channel	Station Called	Location / Remarks	Operator Signature

RADIO LOG

Vessel Name _____   Radio Call Sign _____

Coast Guard VHF Radio Requirements:
1. Must enter each distress (Mayday) message sent **OR** heard.
2. Must enter each urgency (Panpan) for safety (Security) message **you** send.
3. Must enter data on installation and servicing of radio.
4. All entries must be signed by operator.
5. Must retain Radio Log one year minimum from last entry.

Date	Time	Channel	Station Called	Location / Remarks	Operator Signature

RADIO LOG

Vessel Name _____   Radio Call Sign _____

Coast Guard VHF Radio Requirements:
1. Must enter each distress (Mayday) message sent **OR** heard.
2. Must enter each urgency (Panpan) for safety (Security) message **you** send.
3. Must enter data on installation and servicing of radio.
4. All entries must be signed by operator.
5. Must retain Radio Log one year minimum from last entry.

Date	Time	Channel	Station Called	Location / Remarks	Operator Signature

RADIO LOG

Vessel Name _____   Radio Call Sign _____

Coast Guard VHF Radio Requirements:
1.   Must enter each distress (Mayday) message sent **OR** heard.
2.   Must enter each urgency (Panpan) for safety (Security) message **you** send.
3.   Must enter data on installation and servicing of radio.
4.   All entries must be signed by operator.
5.   Must retain Radio Log one year minimum from last entry.

Date	Time	Channel	Station Called	Location / Remarks	Operator Signature

RADIO LOG

Vessel Name _____   Radio Call Sign _____

Coast Guard VHF Radio Requirements:
1. Must enter each distress (Mayday) message sent **OR** heard.
2. Must enter each urgency (Panpan) for safety (Security) message **you** send.
3. Must enter data on installation and servicing of radio.
4. All entries must be signed by operator.
5. Must retain Radio Log one year minimum from last entry.

Date	Time	Channel	Station Called	Location / Remarks	Operator Signature

RADIO LOG

Vessel Name _____ Radio Call Sign _____

Coast Guard VHF Radio Requirements:
1. Must enter each distress (Mayday) message sent **OR** heard.
2. Must enter each urgency (Panpan) for safety (Security) message **you** send.
3. Must enter data on installation and servicing of radio.
4. All entries must be signed by operator.
5. Must retain Radio Log one year minimum from last entry.

Date	Time	Channel	Station Called	Location / Remarks	Operator Signature

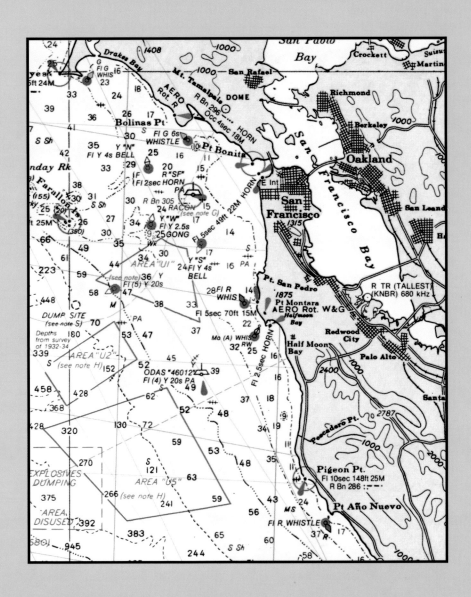

VESSEL INVENTORY — EMERGENCY EQUIPMENT

Date Purchased	Description	Location on Board

The U.S. Coast Guard provides free to anyone a pamphlet titled "Federal Requirements for Recreational Boats."

VESSEL INVENTORY — EMERGENCY EQUIPMENT

Date Purchased	Description	Location on Board

The U.S. Coast Guard provides free to anyone a pamphlet titled "Federal Requirements for Recreational Boats."

VESSEL INVENTORY — SPARE PARTS

Date Purchased	Description	Location on Board

The U.S. Coast Guard provides free to anyone a pamphlet titled "Federal Requirements for Recreational Boats."

VESSEL INVENTORY — SPARE PARTS

Date Purchased	Description	Location on Board

The U.S. Coast Guard provides free to anyone a pamphlet titled "Federal Requirements for Recreational Boats."

VESSEL INVENTORY — LIGHTS

Location of Spare Bulbs:

Location of Bulb	Type	Notes (Tools needed to change bulb)

VESSEL INVENTORY — LIGHTS

Location of Spare Bulbs:

Location of Bulb	Type	Notes (Tools needed to change bulb)

VESSEL INVENTORY — GENERAL

Date Purchased	Cost	Item	Make / Model	Serial Number

VESSEL INVENTORY — GENERAL

Date Purchased	Cost	Item	Make / Model	Serial Number

VESSEL INVENTORY — GENERAL

Date Purchased	Cost	Item	Make / Model	Serial Number

VESSEL INVENTORY — GENERAL

Date Purchased	Cost	Item	Make / Model	Serial Number

VESSEL INVENTORY — GENERAL

Date Purchased	Cost	Item	Make / Model	Serial Number

VESSEL INVENTORY — GENERAL

Date Purchased	Cost	Item	Make / Model	Serial Number

NOTES

NOTES